T0124183

The Mercurial Wandering of My Mind

The Mercurial Wandering of My Mind

Starting Over

REGINA ANDERSON

THE MERCURIAL WANDERING OF MY MIND STARTING OVER

iUniverse books may be ordered through booksellers or by contacting:

iUniverse
1663 Liberty Drive
Bloomington, IN 47403
www.iuniverse.com
1-800-Authors (1-800-288-4677)

Because of the dynamic nature of the Internet, any web addresses or links contained in this book may have changed since publication and may no longer be valid. The views expressed in this work are solely those of the author and do not necessarily reflect the views of the publisher, and the publisher hereby disclaims any responsibility for them.

Any people depicted in stock imagery provided by Thinkstock are models, and such images are being used for illustrative purposes only. Certain stock imagery © Thinkstock.

ISBN: 978-1-5320-2552-5 (sc)
ISBN: 978-1-5320-2553-2 (e)

Library of Congress Control Number: 2017908899

Print information available on the last page.

iUniverse rev. date: 06/13/2017

A Bridge

September 14, 2015

There is something about a bridge,

I always want to cross over,

but then I stop halfway

and gaze into the water,

for hours

in contemplation.

I do not see the water flow

or see the fish swimming.

I am caught always by the sunlight

as it sparkles and shines on the tiny ripples

of the moving water.

I am mesmerized by the dancing,

shimmering reflections of the leaves

captured

on the watery canvas,

and the silvery lined clouds moving

as they slowly drift away.

Memories

October 18, 2015

Like memories out of time,

reflections on still water shine.

I see what is,

I see what was.

Still there,

lingering,

glowing,

misty,

showing.

My memories are drifting,

slowly,

slowly,

turning.

They are rolling through my mind.

Walking Alone

November 21, 2015

I am walking alone

on the quiet shore.

A soft breeze is blowing.

Sunlight is glowing,

glistening on the water.

Waves are rippling,

softly whispering,

as I am walking

alone

on the shore.

My Dream

November 30, 2015

I see you nightly

in my dreams.

Your eyes so dark,

your voice is kind.

You speak to me softly,

letting me know

that we will be together.

I believe you.

I trust you.

Your touch is like feathers,

soft on my face.

Love shines from your eyes,

as you drift away.

Thinking

October 9, 2016

There is a song I would listen to

and at the time the words to me

rang so true.

Now I know these words were a lie.

The pain I feel just will not die.

An ocean is growing, from my tears that are flowing.

How can it be that sad bad memories are so strong?

Those memories came flooding back, with all the emotions

and force.

This is how I feel today.

When you take a rock and throw it not much happens to

the rock.

If you hit it with a sledge-hammer it will certainly crack,

if you hit it more than once you get a pile of chipped broken

rock.

I am not the same person I was before.

I feel like the broken chipped rock.

Little pieces of me are lying everywhere.

Is there a way to put the pieces back
together?
I am waiting for some happy memories,
to wash away all the painful ones.
Please let this be again for me,
I want MY LIFE BACK.

Depression

Nov 7, 2016

My eyes,

the windows of my soul.

I am weeping silent tears and

no one seems to know.

I am hidden behind my door.

I am closed off inside my room.

I am trying to stay safe but

it feels so like a tomb.

What it feels like

TRAPPED

in your own mind.

My soul

April 12, 2016

There is a fire deep inside me.

It is my burning soul.

It is on a mission.

It is on a goal.

It is flaming with desire.

It is shining ever bright.

It is on a search guided by its own light.

The longing is strong.

The need is great.

The moonlight shows the way I take.

It is for you I seek, for you I long.

From dusk till dawn

the search goes on.

I will not stop.

I will not tire.

For you I search

my hearts desire.

Longing

Nov 15, 2016

In the darkest hours of my life

I cry my tears and beg from God.

For good or bad, for wrong or right,

please, just bring me home.

I am so weary of this life.

I am so weary of the strife.

You gave me children and family too,

and took them back with you.

I am not sure just why I am here,

which lessons I have not learned.

With each passing year

I only know that I am

exhausted and beaten.

I have one wish

when I close my eyes

and I fall asleep.

I hope to see my babies,

my loves,

for a short sweet time.

Then I wake with the new light of dawn

and realize I am still here.

I want to go home.

You

November 10, 2015

With each passing day

with every long night,

I think of you.

The way you look,

your almost smile.

The way you sound

when you are tired.

I feel your pain.

I feel your joy.

I see you now when you are sleeping.

I hear your voice when you are speaking.

You are not here but yes, you are.

You are in my mind and in my heart.

Come with me

Dec. 22, 2015

Come with me, my sweet love,

to the sea.

Be with me on this eve, by my side.

Hand in hand

as we stroll through the sand.

Our souls entwined, of one mind,

happy now for all time.

Walking on a high wire

November 14, 2016

I am walking on a high wire,

thinking I can fly.

Is this a reality or a dream gone awry?

Am I in a dream state my subconscious in control?

Am I asleep for this or am I on a roll?

I am walking on a high wire, thinking I can fly.

I slowly close my eyes and lean,

I am falling to the sky.

As I drift towards the moon,

I see you passing by.

Is this my reality

or my dream in-folding me?

I am walking on a high wire.

I think

it's only

me.

Someone,

please,

wake me

soon.

Life

December 3, 2016

I look out into the world.

I see the fantasy the shining lights,

the dreams of days gone by.

Underneath this glitter glowing

I see the sorrow faintly showing.

Then I wonder why?

We are taught from birth beginning,

to have a dream to make our life.

In this life of earthly living

a lesson learned is done by strife.

As we try to learn these lessons,

some prevail and think of riches

earned by labor unforgiving

by the poor who have no living.

Still others fall into a darkness

never to be seen again,

into a madness with no ending.

For them there is no start,

no true beginning.

Still I wonder why?

Through all this

I have hope.

I make a prayer

to God all giving

that I will not fail.

My mama sighed

January 1, 2017

As a child I would play

out in the dirt for the whole day.

I baked mud pies in the sun.

In my eyes this was such fun.

Oh how mama sighed.

I played in the yard with my cat and dog.

I would offer my mom my snake and frog.

In my ripped torn shirt and my tattered jeans

my mud smudged face could not be seen.

I had a fort that I made

underneath a tree in the shade.

Oh how mama sighed.

My dolls all had a broken leg

or something wrong with their poor head,

because I broke them all just like an egg.

I was bad at playing doctor.

Yes, my mama sighed.

Sir Isaac Newton discovered gravity

but I tell you now, haha, that it was Me!

With dire results as you will see,

as I added some velocity.

Oh how mama sighed.

When on one dark and stormy day

I did go outside, but not to play.

With history class still in my head

I tried to be Ben Franklin.

I had my kite with key tied on

and lightning was a crackling.

My kite was high up in the sky

when mama came home,

Oops, a little more than shocking.

Oh my mama sighed.

I will not lie,

I got butt whipped a few good times

for some I know, supposed crimes.

Never once did I shed a tear.

Which shows you all I had no fear.

Yes my mama sighed.

If I fell down and skinned my knees

while riding roller blades.

I never once ever cried.

I would look down at the large band aids

and wear them with great pride.

Oh how mama sighed.

Mama had four girls

but her one desire

was for a boy.

I think she got her one desire,

I was that boy

but with more style.

Yes my mama sighed !!!!

Hopeful

Feb 28, 2017

I am blowing in the wind.

I am chasing the sun into the darkness.

I hear the call of ravens.

My heart beats in fear,

or is it anticipation?

I feel like I have been here,

before,

eons ago.

Is this the end

or another new beginning?

I do not know.

In my journey through this life,

I will continue to chase the sun.

In this never ending cycle,

until my time is done.

Dance with me

I can dance and I am free.

The music plays, my body sways.

I feel the rhythm, I feel the beat.

Yet here I stand so all alone.

Oh won't you please, someone, dance with me?

I see a smile, is it for me?

Your hand is out.

You come this way.

No, you chose another.

I know how to dance.

If I am not chosen,

I can dance

Alone.

I can dance to the music,

to the rhythm, to the flow.

My body moves all on it's own,

all by myself across the room.

Around the floor my body sways,

the music plays and I am free.

I need no one to

dance with

ME!

A mothers Prayer to her child

March 20, 2017

As your mother I will say,

I know how this feels.

I have done my time.

I have seen those views.

My life was full of so much sorrows.

I would close my eyes and cry for hours.

You need a nest a safe place guarded

to bide your time and find the flowers.

Please take your time and snuggle deep,

I swear it helps to get some sleep.

When you wake to each new day dawning,

kiss your love and start by yawning.

Each new day will seem life ending

but as you go you will see the new beginning.

Do not lose hope there is so much joy,

the hard times come so you can learn

and then enjoy all the good that

is to follow.

Kisses

Lost but not Missing

April 10, 2017

I will admit to going lost.

There is a peace that I find

in my lost place.

Do not try so hard to bring me back here,

to this real place of yours.

Your reality is not mine.

I go into my lost place, to find peace.

The solace in this place of mine, brings me comfort.

It is a dark and sometimes lonely place.

There is no excess noise,

no fighting, no screaming,

no laughing, just dark and quiet.

I am here for hours, days, weeks.

I am lost in my own time.

I am finding my own path.

If you stumble upon me here,

listen to the music, the rhythm of my soul,

not the words coming from my mouth.

Look into my eyes,

see my pain, hold my hand,

but please, please,

do not

take me back to the reality

that I am not quite ready

to face at this time.

Leave me be

until I come back on my own.

Ripples

February 12, 2017

Like the butterfly effect,

what you say or do,

changes everything.

The smile you give your wife and child,

at the start of each new day.

When your child asks and you go out and play.

The door you hold for a mother of three.

The kiss you give on bended knee.

Each act is a beginning.

Each and everything you do

causes a rippling in the universe.

Something to think about.

Spring Days

May 12, 2015

I love to go out in my garden

after a long night of rain.

I shake the rain drops off my roses and other flowers.

I think it gives them a little head start on the day.

As the sun comes out they proudly lift their heads up to

offer their nectar to the bees,

butterflies and hummingbirds.

I love to sit in my garden,

it is a peaceful place to think about

life.

Moonlight Dancing

April 15, 2017

When the moon comes out full and bright,

I love to go out late in the night.

I dance to the rhythms in side my soul.

I dance with abandon and no control.

Wild and crazy, whirling and swaying.

No one is watching, no one is waiting.

I lift my arms up to the moon,

my body sways and I could swoon.

The music I choose is inside of me.

The rhythm is strong no need to see.

I sing out loud in a voice made strong,

at this time I can do no wrong.

The pull of the moon is in my very soul.

When I finish, totally spent,

I say my farewell in a good long howl.

Fond memories

April 16, 2017

The meaning of time is non-existent to small children.

They eat and sleep when they please.

Their day consists of play and self-taught learning.

My own children would talk to each other

in some made up language

and act out little life plays.

I tried very hard to put them on a schedule,

to no avail.

Food would be cooked and set on the table.

They fell asleep with their little heads in their plates.

My own bed time would come with total exhaustion.

They were ready for a night on the town.

Go figure, they slept through dinner.

Printed in the United States
By Bookmasters